Big
ELEPHANTS
are useful

❖◉❖

A COMPENDIUM OF
MNEMONICS & IDIOMS

By S J Hartland

Brown Dog Books

Acknowledgements

Thank you to the worldwide web, friends and family for their invaluable help with research.

ISBN 978 19030 56288

First published in the UK in 2008 by
Brown Dog Books
Bath BA2 3LR

Designed by Julia King

Illustrations by Del Thorpe

Produced in the UK

Printed in Malta

A proportion of the profits from this book will be donated to the MS Society (Registered Charity 207495)

Contents

Mnemonic *(nê mon´ik)*.

A memory aid, something that jogs your memory maybe in verse or an amusing saying. Particularly useful for difficult spellings, mathematical rules, geographical and historical facts.

Spelling

Accept
I would ***accept*** your excuse ***except*** the part about losing your watch

Accommodate
Is large enough to ***accommodate*** both two 'c's and two 'm's

Accommodation
There are two <u>c</u>aravans and two <u>m</u>otels

Adolescents and adolescence
The trouble with **adolescen<u>ts</u>** is they never grow out of **adolescen<u>ce</u>**

Affect
To remember when to use **affect** or **effect**
Raven – <u>R</u>emember, **<u>A</u>ffect <u>V</u>**erb, **<u>E</u>ffect <u>N</u>**oun

Allude and elude
I often ***allude*** to my childhood when I remember how I used to ***elude*** my sister in a game of hide and seek

5

Arguement or argument?
> I lost an *'e'* in an ***argument***

Arithmetic <u>A</u> <u>R</u>at <u>I</u>n <u>T</u>he <u>H</u>ouse <u>M</u>ay <u>E</u>at <u>T</u>om's <u>I</u>ce <u>C</u>ream

Ascertain When you ascertain a fact, be ***as certain*** as you possibly can

Assume Never assume as it makes an ***ass*** out of ***u*** and ***me***

❖◈❖◈❖◈❖◈❖◈❖◈❖◈❖◈❖◈❖◈❖

Bare You use a ***bar*** of soap on your ***bare*** skin…..

Bear A ***bear*** can put ***fear*** into you

Beautiful

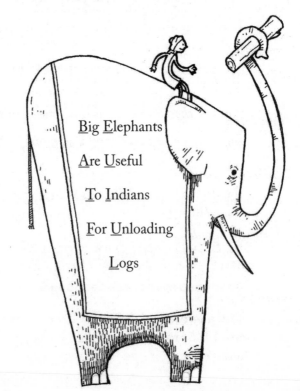

<u>B</u>ig <u>E</u>lephants

<u>A</u>re <u>U</u>seful

<u>T</u>o <u>I</u>ndians

<u>F</u>or <u>U</u>nloading

<u>L</u>ogs

Because	<u>B</u>ig <u>E</u>lephants <u>C</u>an <u>A</u>lways <u>U</u>nderstand <u>S</u>mall <u>E</u>lephants
Believe	Contains a *<u>lie</u>*
Bookkeeper	Remember '*oo kk ee*'
Bicycle	Don't ride your *<u>bicycle</u>* in *<u>icy</u>* weather

❖◇❖◇❖◇❖◇❖◇❖◇❖◇❖◇❖◇❖◇❖◇❖

Calendar	For the correct ending remember, <u>D</u>aughters of the <u>A</u>merican <u>R</u>evolution
Or...	It has an 'e' between two 'a's
Cemetery	Three 'e's are buried in a *ce<u>m</u>e<u>t</u>ery*
Or...	Remember the three 'e's as three tombstones in a graveyard
Choose	There are two options to *ch<u>oo</u>se* from (two 'o's)
Chose	Already *ch<u>o</u>sen* so there is only one option (one 'o')
Church	<u>*Ch*</u> on the right, <u>*Ch*</u> on the left and <u>*ur*</u> in the middle
Committee	Likes to group up all the letters it possibly can
Could, Would, Should	Always end in <u>O</u>ranges <u>U</u>p <u>L</u>emons <u>D</u>own

❖◇❖◇❖◇❖◇❖◇❖◇❖◇❖◇❖◇❖◇❖◇❖

Definite	Has two 'i's *<u>in it</u>*

Dessert   Is a <u>S</u>trawberry <u>S</u>hortcake whilst a de<u>s</u>ert is just <u>S</u>andy

Diarrhoea <u>D</u>ining <u>I</u>n <u>A</u> <u>R</u>ough <u>R</u>estaurant, <u>H</u>urry <u>O</u>therwise <u>E</u>xpect <u>A</u>ccidents!

Or...   <u>D</u>ash <u>I</u>n <u>A</u> <u>R</u>ush, <u>R</u>eally <u>H</u>urry <u>O</u>r <u>E</u>lse <u>A</u>ccident!

Dilemma Emma the *Dil<u>emma</u>*

❖❖❖❖❖❖❖❖❖❖❖❖❖❖❖❖❖❖❖❖

Embarrass You get <u>R</u>eally <u>R</u>ed when you are *embarrassed*

❖❖❖❖❖❖❖❖❖❖❖❖❖❖❖❖❖❖❖❖

February Think... <u>brr</u> it's cold!

Friend or freind?
        Fri<u>end</u> to the <u>end</u>

Geography <u>G</u>eorge <u>E</u>vans' <u>O</u>ld <u>G</u>randmother <u>R</u>ode <u>A</u> <u>P</u>ig <u>H</u>ome <u>Y</u>esterday

Or...   <u>G</u>eorgie <u>E</u>ats <u>O</u>ld <u>G</u>rey <u>R</u>ats <u>A</u>nd <u>P</u>aints <u>H</u>ouses <u>Y</u>ellow

❖❖❖❖❖❖❖❖❖❖❖❖❖❖❖❖❖❖❖❖

Here or hear?
        We h<u>ear</u> with our <u>ear</u>

Hypothesis <u>H</u>eavy <u>Y</u>aks <u>P</u>rance <u>O</u>n <u>T</u>he <u>H</u>ill <u>E</u>very <u>S</u>aturday <u>I</u>n <u>S</u>ummer

❖❖❖❖❖❖❖❖❖❖❖❖❖❖❖❖❖❖❖❖

'I' before 'e' except after 'c' or when sounded like 'a' as in 'neighbour or 'weigh' and weird is just weird!

Independent
The first vowel is 'i' the rest are all 'e's, eeeeeezee

Innocent
<u>In</u> <u>no</u> <u>cent</u>ury is murder an innocent crime

Interrupt
It's <u>R</u>eally <u>R</u>ude to interrupt

Isosceles
<u>I</u> <u>S</u>at <u>O</u>n <u>A</u> <u>S</u>eagull's <u>C</u>liff <u>E</u>ating <u>L</u>ovely <u>E</u>gg <u>S</u>andwiches

❖❖❖❖❖❖❖❖❖❖❖❖❖❖❖❖❖❖❖❖❖

Laugh
<u>L</u>augh <u>A</u>nd <u>U</u> <u>G</u>et <u>H</u>appy

Level
Level is a palindrome and thus well-balanced

License or licence?
S is the verb C is the noun
That's the rule that runs the town
As … The DVLA is *licensed* to issue driving *licences*

❖❖❖❖❖❖❖❖❖❖❖❖❖❖❖❖❖❖❖❖❖

Millennium
Two 'n's and two 'l's then you've spelt it very well
One 'l' or one 'n' then please try again!

Mnemonic
<u>M</u>onkeys <u>N</u>ever <u>E</u>at <u>M</u>ayonnaise <u>O</u>n <u>N</u>oodles <u>I</u>n <u>C</u>anada

❖❖❖❖❖❖❖❖❖❖❖❖❖❖❖❖❖❖❖❖❖

Necessary	One **c**ollar two **s**leeves
Or…	One **c**offee two **s**ugars
Or…	**N**ot **E**very **C**at **E**ats **S**ardines (**S**ome **A**re **R**eally **Y**ummy)

❖❖❖❖❖❖❖❖❖❖❖❖❖❖❖❖❖❖❖❖

Ocean	**O**nly **C**ats' **E**yes **A**re **N**arrow
Ought	**O**swald **U**sually **G**rinds **H**is **T**eeth

❖❖❖❖❖❖❖❖❖❖❖❖❖❖❖❖❖❖❖❖

People	**P**eople **E**at **O**ranges **P**eople **L**ike **E**ating
Perimeter	I can find the ***rim*** in pe***rim***eter
Piece	A **pie**ce of **pie**
Possession	Four sugars so sweet!
Potassium	One **t**ea two **s**ugars

Practise or practice?
Again, remember … S is the verb C is the noun
That's the rule that runs the town
As … A doctor ***practises*** medicine at his ***practice***

Principal	The school princi**pal** is your **pal**
Psychology	**P**lease **S**ay **Y**ou **C**an **H**elp **O**ld **L**adies **O**r **G**obble **Y**oghurt

❖❖❖❖❖❖❖❖❖❖❖❖❖❖❖❖❖❖❖❖

Quizzes   Too many quizzes make me dizzy

Rhythm   <u>R</u>hythm <u>H</u>as <u>Y</u>our <u>T</u>wo <u>H</u>ips <u>M</u>oving

Sculpture   Sculpture is a kind of pic<u>*ture*</u>

Secretary   A <u>*secret*</u>ary can keep a <u>*secret*</u>

Separate   Sep<u>*arat*</u>e is <u>*a rat*</u> of a word to spell

Sheriff   A sheriff has one <u>ri</u>fle but <u>fi</u>res twice

Stationary   St<u>a</u>ying put ends in 'ary'

Stationery   L<u>e</u>tters ends in 'ery'
Or …
Stationary   As in p<u>a</u>rked c<u>a</u>rs

Stationery   As in l<u>e</u>tters or <u>e</u>nvelopes

Success   Double the 'c' double the 's' and you will always have '*success*'!

❖❖❖❖❖❖❖❖❖❖❖❖❖❖❖❖❖❖❖

Together   Remember, *to-get-her*

Tomorrow   <u>T</u>rails <u>O</u>f <u>M</u>y <u>O</u>ld <u>R</u>ed <u>R</u>ose <u>O</u>ver <u>W</u>indow

Too   Has <u>*too*</u> many o's

❖❖❖❖❖❖❖❖❖❖❖❖❖❖❖❖❖❖❖

Wednesday <u>W</u>e <u>D</u>o <u>N</u>ot <u>E</u>at Soup <u>Day</u>

To remember which name is male and which female....

Francis   H<u>i</u>m

Frances   H<u>e</u>r

Language & Grammar

Every name is called a noun,
As <u>field</u> and <u>fountain</u>, <u>street</u> and <u>town</u>.

In place of noun the pronoun stands,
As <u>he</u> or <u>she</u> can clap their hands.

The adjective describes a thing,
As <u>magic</u> wand and <u>bridal</u> ring.

The verb means action, something done,
To <u>read</u> and <u>write</u>, <u>jump</u> and <u>run</u>.

How things are done the adverb tells,
As <u>quickly</u>, <u>slowly</u>, <u>badly</u>, <u>well</u>.

The preposition shows relation,
As <u>in</u> the street or <u>at</u> the station.

Conjunctions join in many ways,
Sentences, words <u>or</u> phrase <u>and</u> phrase.

The interjection cries out 'Hark'!
I need an exclamation mark.

Through poetry, we learn how each
Of these make up the parts of speech.

When two vowels go walking, the first does the talking

As in 'b<u>oa</u>t' or 'p<u>ie</u>'

Six short vowels

Th<u>a</u>t p<u>e</u>n <u>i</u>s n<u>o</u>t m<u>u</u>ch g<u>oo</u>d

Six long vowels

P<u>a</u> m<u>a</u>y w<u>e</u> <u>a</u>ll g<u>o</u> t<u>oo</u>?

Conjunctions

<u>F</u>or, <u>A</u>nd, <u>N</u>or, <u>B</u>ut, <u>O</u>r, <u>Y</u>et, <u>S</u>o
Fanboys

Any word that fits in the blank of this sentence is a preposition

The squirrel ran …….. the tree (over, under, around etc)

To type or write every letter of the alphabet

The Quick Brown Fox
Jumps Over the Lazy Dog

There or Their?

> There is, there are, there were but,
> If it is <u>theirs</u> they are <u>heir</u> to it

Brought and Bought

> *She <u>brought</u> with her all her bargains that she*
> *had recently <u>bought</u> at the market*

When to use less and when to use fewer

> *Less of a lump and fewer 'fings'*

(I must eat less bread and fewer biscuits)

Rob and steal can be confusing, so just remember,

> *You can rob Rob and you can steal steel*
> *But you can't steal Rob and you can't rob steel.*

(You can rob a person and steal something but not the other way round)

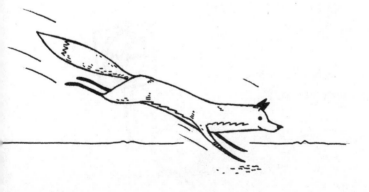

Writing

Less is more

> Don't qualify a statement unless you have to

Grammar matters but style matters more

Remember 'SEX'

> State (S)
> Explain (E)
> Explore (Ex)

This can be used for a whole piece of writing or for its parts i.e. each chapter or paragraph.

Faithfully or Sincerely

> Never two's's together

> Dear Sir,
> Yours faithfully

> Dear Mr Brown
> Yours sincerely

The Solar System

Order of Planets

Mars, Venus, Earth, Mercury, Jupiter, Saturn, Uranus, Neptune Pluto.

>*<u>M</u>y <u>V</u>ery <u>E</u>asy <u>M</u>ethod <u>J</u>ust <u>S</u>peeded <u>U</u>p <u>N</u>aming <u>P</u>lanets*

Or…

>*<u>M</u>y <u>V</u>ery <u>E</u>ducated <u>M</u>other <u>J</u>ust <u>S</u>erved <u>U</u>s <u>N</u>ine <u>P</u>izzas*

Or…

>*<u>M</u>ary <u>V</u>irginia <u>E</u>ats <u>M</u>any <u>J</u>am <u>S</u>andwiches <u>U</u>nder <u>N</u>ellie's <u>P</u>orch*

Or perhaps…

>*<u>M</u>y <u>V</u>ery <u>E</u>xcellent <u>M</u>ethod, <u>J</u>ust <u>S</u>ay <u>Y</u>ou <u>K</u>now <u>P</u>lanets!*

However since Pluto has been demoted to a dwarf planet …..

>*<u>M</u>y <u>V</u>ery <u>E</u>ager <u>M</u>other <u>J</u>ust <u>S</u>erved <u>U</u>s <u>N</u>achos*

Or…

>*<u>M</u>y <u>V</u>ery <u>E</u>xotic <u>M</u>istress <u>J</u>ust <u>S</u>howed <u>U</u>p <u>N</u>aked*

Jupiter's Moons

An Ice-cube Ever Grows Colder

> Amalthea, Io, Europa, Ganymede, Callisto

Neptune's Moons

Neptune's Tiny Dancing Girls Look Pretty Nice Tonight

> Naiad, Thalassa, Despina, Galatea, Larissa, Proteus, Nereid, Triton

(NB Newly discovered ones haven't been named yet)

Phases of the Moon

> *DOC*

D is the waxing moon (1st quarter moon looks like the letter 'D')

O is the full moon (full looks like 'O')

C is the waning moon (3rd quarter looks like the letter 'C')

Weather

> *Rainbow in the morning travellers take warning*
> *Rainbow at night, traveller's delight!*

Or…

> *Red sky at night shepherd's delight*
> *Red sky in the morning shepherd's warning*

Or…

> *Cold is the night when the stars shine bright*

Or…

> *Rain before seven*
> *Fine before eleven*

Or…

> *When grass is dry in morning light*
> *Look for rain before the night*

And not forgetting …

> *The louder the frog the more the rain*

History

Christopher Columbus

> *In Fourteen hundred and ninety-two*
> *Columbus sailed the ocean blue*

The Great Fire of London (1666)

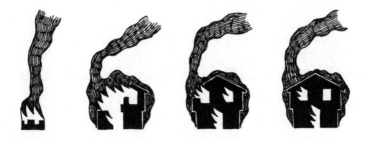

Flight

The first successful flight

In 1903 the Wright brothers flew free

Six Wives of King Henry VIII

> Catherine of Aragon
> Anne Boleyn
> Jane Seymour
> Anne of Cleves
> Catherine Howard
> Katherine Parr

Kate an' Anne an' Jane
An' Anne an' Kate (again, again!)

> And what became of them…

Divorced, Beheaded, Died,
Divorced, Beheaded, Survived

Monarchs of Britain from William the Conqueror

> *Willy, Willy, Harry, Stee,*
> *Harry, Dick, John, Harry three,*
> *One two three Neds, Richard two*
> *Harrys four, five, six, then who?*
> *Edwards four and five, Dick the bad…*
> *Harry's twain, Ned six (the lad)*
> *Mary, Bessie, James you ken.*
> *Then Charlie, Charlie, James again.*
> *Will and Mary, Anna Gloria,*
> *Georges four, Will four, Victoria.*
> *Edward seven next, and then*
> *Came George the fifth in 1910.*
> *Ned the eighth soon abdicated*
> *Then George the sixth was coroneted*
> *After which, Elizabeth…*
> *And that's all folks until her death.*

Ruling Houses of England

Norman, Plantagenet, Lancaster, York, Tudor, Stuart, Hanover, Windsor

No Point Letting Your Trousers Slip Half-Way

Or...

No Plan Like Yours To Study History Wisely

Rank Order

British rank order below Kings and Queens

Do Men Ever Visit Britain?

Duke Marquis Earl Viscount Baron

The Order of Admiral Lord Nelson's Injuries

EARS

Eye, arm, right (x 2)

Admiral Lord Nelson partially lost the sight in his right eye 1794 and then lost his right arm in 1797.

Guy Fawkes

Remember remember the fifth of November,
Gunpowder, treason and plot.
I see no reason why gunpowder treason,
Should ever be forgot.

Guy Fawkes, Guy Fawkes, 'twas his intent,
To blow up King and Parliament.
Three score barrels were laid below,
Poor old England to overthrow.

By God's mercy he was catched,
With a dark lantern and lighted match.
Holler boys, holler boys, let the bells ring,
Holler boys, holler boys, God Save the King!

Seven Deadly Sins

WAGES PL
     <u>W</u>rath, <u>A</u>varice, <u>G</u>luttony, <u>E</u>nvy, <u>S</u>loth, <u>P</u>ride, <u>L</u>ust

Or…

> *I'm very slow to Anger*
> *Don't Envy what you gain*
> *I'm not into Gluttony*
> *I'm not really Vain*
> *Steeped in Lust and Avarice*
> *Yes I could be both*
> *But of all the deadly sins*
> *My favourite is Sloth*

Or perhaps …

     <u>A</u>ll <u>P</u>rivate <u>C</u>olleges <u>L</u>eave <u>S</u>erious <u>E</u>ducational <u>G</u>aps

Anger, Pride, Covetousness, Lust, Sloth, Envy, Greed

The Classical World

Greek Philosophers

The three main Greek philosophers

Greek SPA

Socrates Plato Aristotle

Seven Wonders of the Ancient World

Seems Like Mum Picked Her Toes Continuously

Statue of Zeus
Lighthouse of Alexandria
Mausoleum at Halicarnassus
Pyramid of Khufu
Hanging Gardens of Babylon
Temple of Diana
Colossus of Rhodes

Seven Hills of Rome

Poor Queen Victoria Eats Crow At Christmas

Palatine, Quirinal, Viminal, Esquiline, Capitoline,
Aventine, Caelian

Roman Numerals

<u>I</u> <u>V</u>alue <u>X</u>ylophones <u>L</u>ike <u>C</u>ows <u>D</u>ig <u>M</u>ilk

I	V	X	L	C	D	M
1	5	10	50	100	500	1000

Or..

M's 'mille' (or 1000 said)
D's half (500 – quickly read!)
C's just 100 (century!)
And L is half again – 50!
So all that's left is X and V
(Or 10 and 5) and 1 – easy!

The Natural World

Stalagmites & Stalactites

Stalagmites point ground upwards
Stalactites point ceiling downwards

Or…

> *Tights always fall down*

Or…

> *The mites go up and the tights come down*

Or…

> *A stalagmite might have been a stalactite*
> *If only it had held tight*

Plants

Poison ivy

> *Leaves of three, let it be,*
> *Berries white, take flight*

Snakes

Harmful or not?

> *Red and yellow hurts a fellow*
> *Red and black, friend of Jack*

Rooks & Crows

How do you tell the difference between a rook and a crow?

*If you see a rook on its own it is a crow
and if you see several crows together they are rooks.*

Camels

*<u>B</u>actrian camels have two humps like the letter '<u>B</u>'
<u>D</u>romedary camels have one hump like the letter '<u>D</u>'*

African & Indian Elephants

India's big and its elephant there features,
But Africa's bigger, with much bigger creatures.

Or..

India's big but Africa's bigger
The same as their elephants – easy to figure!

Classification of Living Things

<u>K</u>ings <u>P</u>lay <u>C</u>ards <u>O</u>n <u>F</u>airly <u>G</u>ood <u>S</u>oft <u>V</u>elvet

Or…

<u>K</u>indly <u>P</u>lace <u>C</u>over <u>O</u>n <u>F</u>resh <u>G</u>reen <u>Sp</u>ring <u>V</u>egetables

Or…

*Krakatoa Positively Casts Off Fumes Generating
Sulphurous Vapours*

Kingdom, Phylum, Class, Order, Family, Genus, Species,
Variety

Classification for Humans

Anthropology Can Make People Hate Helping the Sick
> Animalia, Chordata, Mamalia, Primate, Hominidae,
> Homo Sapiens

Vertebrates

For the five classes of vertebrates in the animal kingdom,
just think

Farm Birds

> Fish
> Amphibians
> Reptiles
> Mammals
> Birds

Or…

> *Barfm!*

Handy Hints

Eating Shellfish

Never eat shellfish in month without an 'r'

How to Avoid Stomach Upsets when Travelling Abroad

Peel it, boil it or forget it!

Alcohol

Beer on whisky? Very risky!
Whisky on beer? Never fear!

Or…

Wine on beer makes you queer
Beer on wine makes you feel fine

In the Kitchen

Vinaigrette dressing:

Be a counsellor with the salt
A miser with the vinegar
And a spendthrift with the oil

A common mistake is to add too much vinegar.

Left & Right

You can make the letter 'L' with your left hand

Remedies for Insect Stings

Use Ammonia for a Bee sting
And Vinegar for a Wasp sting

<u>A</u> followed by <u>B</u>
<u>V</u> followed by <u>W</u>

Changing the Clocks for British Summertime

Spring Forwards

Fall Backwards

Or...

Into Summer
Back to Winter

Number of Days in each Month

Thirty days hath September, April, June and November.
All the rest have thirty-one except for February
Which has 28 days clear and 29 each Leap Year.

Tightening a Screw

Righty tighty, lefty loosey

Taps & Valves

Clockwise is closing

Wiring a Plug

The live brown bear,
Looked at the neutral blue sky,
From the green and yellow earth.

Or…

Blue to the left,
Brown to the right,
What remains goes up the middle.

Or…

Brown is hot,
Blue is not,
Green and yellow,
Earth the lot!

Clothing

Which way should men and women button jackets?

> *Women are always right*

Or….

> *Men are leftovers!*

Tying a Tie

> *The big guy is always right*

The larger end hangs down the right side of your neck

How to Shoot a Rifle

> *Brass*

<u>B</u>reathe, <u>r</u>elax, <u>a</u>im, <u>s</u>ight, <u>s</u>queeze

Ceilidh Dancing

To remember on which side the woman stands

> *Women like to be right*

Burning Firewood

Beech wood fires are bright and clear
If the logs are kept a year;
Chestnut's only good, they say,
If for long 'tis laid away;
Make a fire of elder tree,
Death within your home shall be;
But ash new or ash old,
Is fit for Queen with crown of gold.

Birch and fir logs burn too fast,
Blaze up bright and do not last;
It is by the Irish said,
Hawthorn bakes the sweetest bread;
Elmwood burns like churchyard mould,
E'en the very flames are cold;
But ash green or ash brown
Is fit for Queen with golden crown.

Poplar gives a bitter smoke,
Fills your eyes and makes you choke;
Apple wood will scent your room,
With an incense like perfume;
Oaken logs, if dry and old,
Keep away the winter's cold;
But ash wet or ash dry
A king shall warm his slippers by.

Signs of the Zodiac

Aries Taurus Gemini Cancer Leo Virgo Libra Scorpio
Sagittarius Capricorn Aquarius Pisces

> *All The Great Constellations Live Very Long Since Stars
> Can't Alter Physics*

Or..

> *A Tense Grey Cat Lay Very Low Sneaking Slowly
> Contemplating A Pounce*

Or even …

> *The Ram, the Bull and the Heavenly Twins
> And next the Crab, the Lion shines,
> The Virgin and the Scales
> The Scorpion, Archer and He-Goat
> The Man that carries the Watering Pot
> And the Fish with the glittering tails.*

Mathematics & Measurements

Calculations

Order of operations in maths

> Parenthesis, exponents, multiplication, division, addition and subtraction

> _Please Excuse My Dear Aunt Sally_

Long Division

Divide, multiply, subtract, bring down
To remember this order, use the following phrases:

> _Dead Monkeys Smell Bad_

Or…

> _Dad Mother Sister Brother_

Greater & Less Than

> _The crocodile's mouth always opens towards the larger meal (number)_

3 < 7   The crocodile wants to eat 7, therefore 3 is less than 7
5 > 2   The crocodile wants to eat 5, therefore 5 is greater than 2

Subtraction Borrowing

Just remember…

> *Bigger Bottom*
> *Better Borrow*

Metric System

King Hector Doesn't Usually Drink Cold Milk

Kilo	1000
Hecto	100
Deca	10
Units	0
Deci	.01
Centi	.001
Milli	.0001

Temperature

The Celsius scale

> *30 is hot*
> *20 is nice*
> *10 is cold*
> *And 0 is ice!*

Or…

> *When it's zero it's freezing*
> *When it's 10 it's not*
> *When it's 20 it's warm*
> *When it's 30 it's hot!*

Measurements

For those of us who still think in imperial measurements…

> *A litre of water's a pint and three quarters*

And …

> *A metre measures three foot three, it's longer than*
> *a yard you see*

Or, in America. …

> *Two CUPS make a PINT*
> *And two PINTS make a QUART*
> *But you'll never get a GALLON*
> *Unless you add FOUR QUARTS*

Pi (the first few digits)

The numbers of the letters in each word gives the digits of Pi

> *How I wish I could calculate Pi*

> 3.141592

Or…

> *May I have a large container of coffee?*

> 3.1415926

Or perhaps…

> How I love a white Christmas

> 3.14159

Geography

Location of Sicily

Long legged Italy
Kicked poor Sicily
Into the Mediterranean Sea!

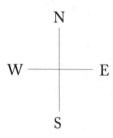

Points of the Compass

Never Eat Shredded Wheat

Or...

Never Eat Salty Worms

Or maybe...

Naughty Elephants Squirt Water

Longitude & Latitude

Latitude – Lines Across (East West) or Latitude *'goes around the equator belt'*

Longitude – Lines top to bottom (North South)

Countries of Central America

My Great Big Elephant Has Nine Chocolate Peanuts

Mexico, Guatemala, Belize, El Salvador, Honduras, Nicaragua, Costa Rica, Panama

The Original 13 States of the USA

My Nice New Car Needs Re-Painting, Maybe Dark Violet? No, Shiny Gold!

Massachusetts
New Hampshire
New York
Connecticut
New Jersey
Rhode Island
Pennsylvania
Maryland
Delaware
Virginia
North Carolina
South Carolina
Georgia

Height of Mount Fujiyama

A year in months and days

> 12,365 feet

Great Lakes of North America

HOMES

> Huron, Ontario, Michigan, Erie, Superior

Counties of Northern Ireland

Don't Take Long, Add Another Fossil

> Down, Tyrone, Londonderry, Antrim, Armagh,
> Fermanagh

The Seven Continents

Eat An Aspirin After A Night-time Snack

> Europe, Antarctica, Asia, Africa, Australia,
> North America, South America

The Four Oceans

I Am A Person

> Indian, Arctic, Atlantic, Pacific

Months of the Caribbean Hurricane Season

June - Too soon (first month)

July - Standby (for news of the storm)

August - You must (get prepared in case of storm)

September - Remember (to standby)

October – It's all over (last month)

Carpal Bones

Carpenters use their hands so *carpal* bones are of the hand not foot.

Wrist Bones

There are eight carpal bones

> Scaphoid, lunate, triquetral, pisiform, trapezium, trapezoid, capitate, hamate

> *Some Lovers Try Positions That They Can't Handle*

Or...

> *She Looks Too Pretty Try To Catch Her*

Blood

Functions of blood

> *Old Charlie Foster Hates Women Having Dull Clothes*

> Oxygen (transport), carbon dioxide (transport), food, heat, waste, hormones, disease, clotting

Cardiology

The order of resuscitation for heart sounds from right to left.

> *All Prostitutes Take Money*

> Aortic, pulmonary, tricuspid, mitra

Excretory Organs of the Body

SKILL

Skin, kidneys, intestines, liver, lungs

Three Things Your Circulatory System Has to 'Have'

<u>H</u>eart
<u>A</u>rteries
<u>V</u>eins

Properties of Bile

Bile from the liver emulsifies greases,
Tinges the urine and colours the faeces,
Aids peristalsis prevents putrefaction,
If you remember all this you'll give satisfaction.

Life Processes

Mrs Gren

Movement, respiration, sensitivity, growth, reproduction, excretion, nutrition

Cranial Nerves

*On Old Olympus' Towering Tops
A Finn And German Viewed Some Hops*

Olfactory, optic, oculomotor, trochlear, trigeminal, abducens, facial, acoustic, glosspharyngeal, vagus, spinal, (accessory) hypoglossal

Bones of the Skull

Old People From Texas Eat Spiders

Occipital, parietal, frontal, temporal, ephnoid, sphenoid

Amino Acids

Ten essential amino acids

These Ten Valuable Amino acids Have Long Preserved Life In Man

> Threonine
> Trytophan
> Valine
> Ariginine
> Histidine
> Lysine
> Phenylalanine
> Leucine
> Isoleucine
> Methionine

Elements in the Human Body

C Hopkins' café is mighty good, but take it with a pinch of NaCl

C	=	Carbon
H	=	Hydrogen
P	=	Phosphorous
K	=	Potassium
I	=	Iodine
N	=	Nitrogen
S	=	Sulphur
Ca	=	Calcium
Fe	=	Iron
Mg	=	Magnesium
Na	=	Salt
Cl	=	Chlorine

The Causes of (nearly all) Diseases

TIN VA MEDIC

Trauma, infection, neoplasm, vascular, auto-immune, metabolic, endocrine, degenerative, iatrogenic, congenital

Onset of Rashes and Day of Fever

Very Sick Patients Must Take No Exercise

Varicella (chicken pox)	1st day
Scarlet fever	2nd day
Pox (Smallpox)	3rd day
Measles	4th day
Typhus	5th day
Nothing	6th day
Enteric fever (typhoid)	7th day

Prone & Supine

The difference between *prone* (face down) and *supine* (face up)

> *In muggings muggers must attack*
> *The victim's proper zone,*
> *The belly if he's supine,*
> *And the spine if he is prone.*

Survival

In a survival situation remember…

> *STOP*
> *Stop, Take Inventory, Orientate, Plan*

Minor Injuries

For minor soft tissue injuries such as bruising and muscle strain, remember

> *ICE*
> *Ice, Compression and Elevation*

Prompt application of ice reduces local swelling.

Application of compression bandage and elevation of the part further reduces swelling.

Casualties

To treat a casualty, remember

> *Dr. ABC*
> *Danger, Response, Airways, Breathing, Circulation*

and…

> *AVPU*

Establish the following…

> *Alert, Voice, Pain, Unconscious*

First Aid

Basic rule of thumb in First Aid, **as long as** you do not suspect any spinal injury.

> *Face is red, raise the head,*
> *Face is pale, raise the tail*

BUT remember...

Never attempt anything that you have not been trained to do.

Causes of Coma

Remember...

AEIOU TIPS

A – Alcohol
E – Epilepsy or exposure
I – Insulin (diabetic emergency)
O – Overdose or oxygen deficiency
U – Uraemia (toxins due to kidney failure)
T – Trauma (shock, head injury)
I – Infection
P – Psychosis or poisoning
S – Stroke

Fire Safety

> Get out, stay out, call 999

Or ...

RACE

> *Rescue, Alarm, Contain, Extinguish*

Or...

FIRE

> Find the fire,
> Inform people by shouting or calling,
> Restrict the spread of fire, (if possible and safe to do so),
> Evacuate the area

And...

PASS

> *Pull, Aim, Squeeze and Sweep*
> (when using a fire extinguisher)

Music

Order of Sharps

Fat Cats Get Dizzy After Eating Beans
(FCGDAEB)

Order of Flats

Battle Ends And Down Goes Charlie's Father
(BEADGCF)

Standard Guitar Tuning

Earl's Bible Gets Dusty After Easter
(EBGDAE)

Or…

> _Everybody Gets Drunk At Election_

Notes on the Treble Clef

> _Every Good Boy Deserves Fun_
> (EGBDF)

Notes on the Bass Clef

> _Good Boys Deserve Fun Always_
> (GBDFA)

Quartet

STAB

> Soprano, tenor, alto and baritone, the four voices in a quartet.

Or – in order of pitch

> _Start At The Beginning_

Geology

Geological Ages

Cenozoic Era

From 65 million years ago to today

> *Put Eggs On My Plate Please*
>
> Paleocene, Eocene, Oligocene, Miocene, Pliocene, Pleistocene

Mesozoic Era

248 to 65 million years ago

> *Try Jesus Christ*

Or...

> *Tom Jerry Can*
> Triassic, Jurassic, Cretaceous

Palaeozoic Era

543 to 248 million years ago

> *Can Oscar See Down My Pants Pocket?*
>
> Cambrian, Ordovician, Silurian, Devonian, Mississippian, Pennsylvanian, Permian

Mineral Hardness Scale

Talc, Gypsum, Calcite, Fluorite, Apatite, Orthoclase, Quartz, Topaz, Corundum, Diamond

> The Gem Cutters From Adelaide Often Queue To Cut Diamonds

Or...

> Toronto Girls Can Flirt And Only Quit To Chase Dwarves

The Three Types of Rock

SIM

> Sedimentary, Igneous, Metamorphic

Order of Sizes of Rock Matter

> *Boys Can't Pass Social Studies Class*
>
> Boulder, Cobble, Pebble, Sand, Silt, Clay

Seafaring Safety

When all three lights I see ahead,
I turn to starboard and show my red.
Green to green, red to red,
Perfect safety, go ahead!

Port & Starboard

To remember which is port and which is starboard

> *When on deck facing the front of the ship port side is to the left, just as at dinner port is traditionally passed to the left*

Or…

> *Port and left have the same number of letters leaving starboard on the right*

Or…

> *Port is a red wine and red is on the left side of politics*
> *Left side of the ship is called port and has a red light*

Or….

> *A little bit of <u>port</u> <u>left</u> in the glass*

Red Right Returning

Mariners use this to remind them that when they are returning from sea into port, red buoys should be kept to the right side of the ship.

If, to your starboard, red appear,
It is your duty to keep clear;
To act as judgement says is proper,
To starboard – or port – back – or stop her.
But when, upon your port, is seen,
A steamer's starboard light of green
There's not so much for you to do,
For green to port keeps clear of you.

Water Depth – Shallow to Deep

Brown, brown, run aground,
White, white you might,
Green, green nice and clean,
Blue, blue run right through!

Working World

Employment

A tight labour market means there are many jobs available.

> *Tell your boss to fly a kite,*
> *When the labour market is tight.*

Seven Functions of Marketing

Did Fred Make Purple Pecan Pie Saturday?

> Distribution
> Finance
> Marketing Information
> Product
> Price
> Place
> Selling

…but remember

ABC

> Be Accurate, Brief and Clear

And…

PPPPP

> *Proper Planning Prevents Poor Performance*

KISS (Keep It Simple Stupid)

French

Exceptions to the rule in French that adjectives should come after the noun

BAGS

    <u>B</u>eauty <u>A</u>ge <u>G</u>oodness <u>S</u>ize

Verbs which require *être* as the auxiliary verb in the *passé composé* instead of *avoir*

    Dr (&) Mrs Vandertrampp

<u>D</u>evenir, <u>r</u>evenir, <u>m</u>ourir <u>r</u>etourner, <u>s</u>ortir, <u>v</u>enir, <u>a</u>ller, <u>n</u>aître, <u>d</u>escendre, <u>e</u>ntrer, <u>r</u>entrer <u>t</u>omber, <u>r</u>ester, <u>a</u>rriver, <u>m</u>onter, <u>p</u>asser, <u>p</u>artir

Science

Mixing Colours (Light)

Better Get Ready When   Primary
                               (<u>B</u>lue <u>G</u>reen <u>R</u>ed = <u>W</u>hite*)*
Your Mistress Comes Back   Secondary
                               (<u>Y</u>ellow <u>M</u>agenta <u>C</u>yan = <u>B</u>lack)

The Colours of the Rainbow

Roy G Biv

Or..

<u>R</u>ichard <u>O</u>f <u>Y</u>ork <u>G</u>ave <u>B</u>attle <u>I</u>n <u>V</u>ain

Red, Orange, Yellow, Green, Blue, Indigo, Violet

Common Magnetic Materials

NICS

Nickel, iron, copper, steel

Oxidation & Reduction

Oxidation takes place at anode
Reduction takes place at cathode

ANode for OXidation   AN OX
REDuction at CAThode RED CAT

Oxidation Is Losing electrons
Reduction Is Gaining electrons

Just remember...

OIL RIG

Brass & Bronze

These are alloys that contain copper, but one contains tin and the other contains zinc.

Which one contains which?

Bronze *does not* contain zinc

Food Groups

Carbohydrate, Proteins, Fats, Minerals, Vitamins, Fibre, Water

Chemistry

Johnny was a chemist
Johnny is no more
Because he thought that H2O was H2SO4!

(H_2O is water, H_2SO_4 is Sulphuric Acid)

Road Safety

Driving a Car

When parking uphill turn your wheels away from the street

Up, up and away

Before moving away from a stationary position, remember

Mirror, signal, manoeuvre

Five 's's

Safety
Smoothness
System (of car control)
Style
Speed

CAT

Concentrate, Anticipate, Tolerate

Brakes for slowing, gears for going

Less space less speed

When a stop becomes a wait apply the handbrake

*If you don't know, **don't go***

Make sure you remember your seatbelt

> *Clunk click every trip*

And when going out for the evening

> *Think, before you drink, before you drive*

Crossing the Road

> *Stop Look Listen*

Or...

> *Stop! Look! Listen! Think!*
> *Everyone repeat!*
> *Stop! Look! Listen! Think!*
> *Before you cross the street!*

Then...

> *Look right, look left, look right again*

And Finally …

Romeo & Juliet

To remember which family each character belongs to,

> *Juliet* belongs to the *Capulet* family and
> *Romeo* belongs to the *Montague* family

U.S. Military

The different ranks of general in the U.S. military (one star to four stars)

> *Be My Little General*

1. Brigadier General
2. Major General
3. Lieutenant General
4. General

The Twelve Disciples

> *Jesus called them one by one,*
> *Peter, Andrew, James and John,*
> *Next, came Philip, Thomas too,*
> *Matthew and Bartholomew.*
>
> *James the one they called the less,*
> *Simon, also Thaddeus,*
> *Twelfth apostle Judas made,*
> *Jesus was by him betrayed.*

The Seven Dwarfs

I was tired and Sneezy
So I went to the Doc
But I felt quite Bashful
Because he wore a frock

He was very Grumpy
Not Happy in the least
Now I'm Sleepy and Dopey
And he's the local priest.

Or..

Two 's's Sleepy & Sneezy
Two 'd's Dopey & Doc
Three emotions Happy, Bashful & Grumpy

Rules for the Bathroom

Please remember, don't forget,
Never leave the bathroom wet.
Nor the soap still in the water,
That's a thing you never oughta'.
Nor leave the towels about the floor,
Nor keep the bath an hour or more,
When other folks are wanting one,
Please don't forget,
This isn't done!

Idioms *(id'eam).*

An accepted phrase having a meaning different from the literal. An expression that is peculiar to itself grammatically.

Idioms are used in every day speech, more often than we realise. The following selection is both traditional and modern, some of which require a short explanation, others which are obvious and speak for themselves. Certain to entertain and amuse!

Love

An old flame *(An old girlfriend or boyfriend)*

He still holds a candle for her
(Someone you still have feelings for)

Wear you heart on your sleeve *(Display your feelings)*

You're the apple of my eye and the star in my sky
(Someone dear to you, usually a father to a daughter)

No man ever wore a scarf as warm as his daughter's arm around his neck

Love is blind *(Overlook a person's faults)*

Let your heart rule your head *(Let your emotions take over)*

The best thing to hold onto in life is each other
(Look after each other)

Better to have loved and lost than never to have loved at all

Have a crush on someone
(Have strong feelings very quickly for someone)

Head over heels in love *(Very much in love)*

A match made in heaven *(A perfect match)*

Marriages are made in heaven

To be loved-up *(Warm feeling of love)*

Marry in Lent, and you'll live to repent

A day without you is like a day without chocolate

No love like the first love

Loved you then, love you still
Always have, always will

Love will find a way

A life alone is not a life worth living

Do you love me or do you not?
You told me once but I forgot

If you love something set it free

Absence makes the heart grow fonder

You rock my world *(You are the best)*

The only cure for love is marriage

Of Limited Intelligence

He's not the sharpest knife in the drawer

One sandwich short of a picnic

He's not playing with a full deck

The lights are on but there is no-one home

The wheel is turning but the hamster is dead

Two pickles short of a quart

A couplet short of a sonnet

A few clowns short of a circus

Has a vacancy on the top floor

The attic's a little dusty

He got into the gene pool when the lifeguard wasn't watching

Not the quickest bunny in the forest

A few fries short of a happy meal

He checked out of Hotel Brainy years ago

Forgot to pay his brain bill

Missing a few buttons on the remote control

As smart as bait

He's as sharp as a marble

He's as sharp as a thimble

When his IQ reaches 50 he should sell

If you stand close enough to him you can hear the sea

All foam no beer

One putt short of a par

He's bungalow Bill *(Hasn't got a top storey)*

A Medley of Similes

As blind as a bat *(Can't see very well)*

As sick as a parrot (*Annoyed*)

As happy as a peacock (*Happy*)

As happy as a pig in muck (*Happy*)

As deaf as a post *(Can't hear very well)*

As smooth as a baby's bottom *(Very smooth)*

As soft as old mick *(Very gentle)*

As high as a kite (*Very excited*)

As mad as a wet hen *(Angry)*

As mad as a March hare *(Completely bonkers)*

As mad as a bag of spanners (*Crazy*)

As fit as a butcher's dog (*Very physically fit*)

As rare as hen's teeth *(Rare)*

As baffled as Adam on Mother's Day (*Baffled*)

As confused as a fart in a perfume factory (*Confused*)

As nervous as a turkey at Christmas *(Nervous)*

As nervous as a pig in a bacon factory *(Nervous)*

As silent as an angel's fart *(Quiet)*

As welcome as a taxman's letter *(Not welcome)*

As steep as a cow's face *(Very steep)*

As clear as mud *(Not clear)*

As much chance as a wax cat in hell *(No chance)*

As conceited as a barber's cat *(Conceited)*

As ugly as sin *(Ugly)*

As mean as a junkyard dog *(Very mean)*

As quick as a dog can lick a dish *(Very quick)*

As crooked as a dog's hind leg *(Dishonest)*

As busy as a fish peddler in Lent *(Very busy)*

As pretty as a speckled pup *(Very pretty)*

As calm as a toad in the sun *(Very calm)*

As white as a sheet *(Very pale complexion)*

As freckled as a turkey egg *(Very freckled)*

Feeling like a rooster in a hen house *(Feeling out of place)*

Wicked!

Sweating like a pig

A pig's breakfast *(A mess)*

Dressed up like a dog's dinner *(Really dressed up)*

Face like a bulldog chewing a wasp

Mouth like a cat's arse

Tight as a duck's arse *(Very careful with money)*

Camp as a row of tents

Queer as a chocolate orange

Queer as a football bat

The tide wouldn't take her out *(Unattractive)*

She fell off the ugly tree and hit every branch on the way down
(Unattractive)

If wit were shit you would be constipated *(Not witty at all)*

Mutton dressed as lamb
(Middle aged or elderly person trying to look younger)

Fur coat and no knickers
(Act with airs and graces but has no real class)

A face only a mother could love

A perfect face for Halloween

Have you lost your marbles? *(Have you gone mad?)*

He's tighter than a photo-finish *(Doesn't spend money easily)*

Nutty as a fruit cake *(Crazy)*

Big enough to choke a cow *(Very big)*

Dog-faced liar *(A terrible liar)*

Sleeping with the fishes *(Watery death)*

Couldn't stop a pig in a passage *(Bowlegged)*

Flip the bird *(Stick up your middle finger in a derogatory way)*

Useless! ✳ ✳ ❋ !

As useless as a carpet fitter's ladder

As much use as a handbrake on a canoe

About as much use as a chocolate teapot

About as much use as an ashtray on a motorbike

Couldn't carry a tune in a bucket *(Musically useless)*

Couldn't fight his way out of a paper bag

As lost as a ball in high weeds

No use to man nor beast

Doesn't have the sense God gave geese

Sorry as owl bait

A dead duck *(Bound to fail)*

Thick as mince

Out to lunch

Dead from the neck up

A fifth wheel

Everyday Expressions

Barking up the wrong tree *(Being wrong, incorrect)*

At the end of my tether *(At the point of frustration)*

At the end of my rope *(As above)*

Two wrongs don't make a right
(It is not right to do wrong to another person, even if they have wronged you)

It's gone to the dogs *(It's not very good any more)*

The early bird catches the worm
(You will get the best choice if you are early)

He's kissed the blarney stone
(Somebody who is charming and witty)

Get a move on! *(Hurry up)*

That's the icing on the cake
(Something good happens on top of something else)

I would give my right arm for that *(I would really like that)*

The cut of your jib *(Your general appearance and demeanour)*

Civility costs nothing and buys everything *(Be civil and it will be to your advantage)*

Below the belt *(Unfair – from boxing)*

Steal your thunder *(Take credit for something inappropriately)*

Whatever floats your boat *(Whatever you like)*

Break the ice *(Start a conversation in a social situation)*

Between you, me and the gatepost *(A secret, keep it to yourself)*

In a nutshell *(Information contained in a few words)*

Go the whole hog *(To do something completely)*

Two shakes of a lamb's tail *(Quickly)*

To have butterflies in your stomach *(To feel nervous)*

Make a pig's ear out of something *(Make a complete mess)*

Bone idle   *(Utterly lazy)*

Away with the fairies *(Not being realistic)*

A lick and a promise *(A quick, hasty wash)*

Start off on the wrong foot *(Start badly)*

Bend over backwards *(Try very hard)*

Butter someone up *(Flatter)*

Take it with a pinch of salt
(Accept it, but maintain a degree of scepticism)

Like a lamb to the slaughter *(Without resistance)*

Chase your tail *(Very busy but not productive)*

Get your feet wet *(Your first experience of something)*

Like a headless chicken
(With no structure or coordination, all over the place)

Familiar Phrases

In a pickle *(In a mess)*

Gone pear-shaped *(Gone wrong)*

Cream of the crop *(The best)*

Not my cup of tea *(Don't really like it)*

Black sheep of the family
(Most troublesome member of the family)

To call a spade a spade *(To speak frankly)*

To put the cart before the horse
(To do something in reverse order)

Every man and his dog *(A lot of people)*

All over bar the shouting *(The outcome is obvious)*

Neck and neck *(Equal)*

No dice *(Absolutely not)*

Bolt from the blue *(Unexpected)*

Bag of nerves *(Very nervous)*

On the back foot *(At a disadvantage)*

If you'll pardon my French *(Apologising for swearing)*

Not to be sneezed at *(To be taken seriously)*

Rub shoulders
(Meet and spend time with a well-known person)

Hit the hay *(Go to bed)*

To learn the hard way *(Have a bad experience)*

Tales of derring-do *(Tales of excitement and courage)*

Forty winks *(A nap)*

Weird ❦ *Wonderful*

Hitch your wagon to a star *(Aim high)*

Keep your eyes peeled *(Watch carefully)*

Make your flesh crawl *(Scares or revolts you)*

Make your toes curl *(To shock or embarrass)*

Snatched the pebble *(Grasped the full meaning)*

All ears   *(Eager to listen)*

At loggerheads *(Quarrelsome)*

In rude health *(In good health)*

Fuss and feathers *(Fancy things)*

The whole shebang *(All of it)*

Pull the fat from the fire
(Help someone in a difficult situation)

Belt and braces *(Leave no room for error)*

Itchy feet   *(Wanting to travel)*

Belly up   *(Things have gone badly wrong)*

It's like nailing jelly to a tree *(Very difficult)*

His ears are flapping *(Trying to hear what is being said)*

His ears are burning
(Someone who is being talked about behind their back)

A baptism of fire *(First experience, often difficult)*

A hitchin' in your giddy-up *(Feeling unwell)*

Moods

Poker faced *(Straight faced to the point of looking displeased)*

A face like thunder *(Looking angry)*

To go ballistic *(Losing your temper)*

He's got the gift of the gab *(Somebody who can talk easily)*

Get out of bed on the wrong side *(In a bad mood)*

At a loose end *(Bored, not sure what to do)*

To have a stiff upper lip *(To be very proper or restrained)*

Beside yourself *(Very intense feeling)*

On tenterhooks *(Anxious)*

To go to pieces *(To be very badly affected by something)*

As cool as a cucumber *(Not worried by anything)*

To be on the warpath *(To be angry)*

To see red *(To be angry)*

To make someone's blood boil *(Make someone very angry)*

Hit the roof *(Be angry)*

Bright-eyed and bushy-tailed *(Eager and alert)*

Mad as a struck snake *(Angry)*

In a fog *(Confused)*

Cheesed-off *(Fed-up)*

Chip on your shoulder *(Resentful about something)*

Cry your eyes out *(Cry uncontrollably)*

Heart in your boots *(Unhappy)*

Sweating bullets *(Very nervous)*

Throw your toys out of the pram *(Angry protest)*

Speak of the Devil

I don't know what the devil you see in her
(I don't know what you see in her)

What the devil did you say? *(Implying it was unbelievable)*

Talk of the devil and he's bound to appear
(Talk about someone and they will appear)

The devil makes work for idle hands
(If a person isn't busy they will find mischief)

Devil-may-care attitude *(Couldn't care less)*

Better the devil you know *(Better than the unknown)*

Until hell freezes over *(For eternity)*

Give the devil his due *(Be fair even if you dislike the person)*

Weather

It's raining cats and dogs *(It's raining heavily)*

It's raining stair rods *(It's raining very heavily)*

You'll catch your death *(You will catch a chill)*

Every cloud has a silver lining
(There's always something good in every problem)

It's hot as a docker's armpit *(Very hot)*

As hot as hell

A scorcher!

Steal someone's thunder
(To take away praise that was due to someone else)

A snowball in hell's chance *(Very little chance)*

Snowed under *(Very busy)*

Under the weather *(Unwell)*

Make heavy weather of something
(Making something seem more difficult than it is)

Any port in a storm *(Any solution will do in an emergency)*

A storm in a teacup *(A fuss about nothing)*

Blow hot and cold *(Keep changing your mind)*

Chase rainbows *(Trying to do something unachievable)*

It never rains but it pours
(If something goes wrong then it goes very wrong)

Tempest in a teapot
(Exaggerating the seriousness of a situation)

Twisting in the wind *(Without help or support)*

Scotch mist *(Hard to find or doesn't exist)*

Eye of the storm *(Centre of the storm)*

Monetary Matters

A fool and his money are soon parted
(Somebody who spends money thoughtlessly is unwise)

Neither a borrower nor a lender be
(Don't lend money or borrow money)

All that glitters is not gold *(May not be as valuable as it seems)*

Rags to riches *(From poor to wealthy)*

You can't take it with you *(Enjoy things while you can)*

It's worth a mint *(Worth a lot of money)*

It cost an arm and a leg *(Cost a lot of money)*

Money doesn't grow on trees *(It doesn't come easily)*

A pretty penny *(It's expensive)*

A penny saved is a penny earned
(Better to be cautious with money)

Penny wise, pound foolish
(Wise with pennies but spend large amounts easily)

When poverty comes in at the door, love flies out of the
window

Poor as a church mouse

It is better to be born lucky than rich

Throwing his money around like a man with no arms
(Being extravagant with money)

Tighten your belt *(To be more careful with money)*

Go Dutch *(Share the cost)*

Hard up *(Very little money)*

Feel the pinch *(Short of money)*

To laugh all the way to the bank *(To make money easily)*

In the red *(In debt)*

A bit steep *(Expensive)*

Daylight robbery *(Not worth the money)*

A steal *(Good value)*

He has deep pockets *(Wealthy)*

Put your money where your mouth is *(Don't just talk about it)*

Make a bundle *(Make a lot of money)*

Make a killing *(Make a lot of money)*

Money to burn *(A lot of money to spend)*

Pad the bill *(Add false expenses)*

Pinch pennies *(Be careful with money)*

Bring home the bacon *(Earn a living for the family)*

Save up for a rainy day
(Put money aside for when it might be needed)

The gravy train
(Ways of making a lot of money without much effort)

Go for broke *(Risk everything)*

Going for a song *(Cheap)*

Pay top dollar *(Pay a lot of money)*

Green stuff *(Money)*

Grease someone's palm *(Bribe someone)*

Live high off the hog *(Have a lot of money to live comfortably)*

Bet your bottom dollar *(Be certain about something)*

Spend a penny *(Visit the lavatory)*

———◆◆———

At work

Back to the drawing board *(Start again)*

Back to square one *(Start again)*

To sink or swim *(To fail or succeed)*

Actions speak louder than words
(Do something rather than just talk about it)

Burning the midnight oil *(Staying up late, working hard)*

I'm staying on the fence *(Not supporting any side of a dispute)*

Do as I say, not as I do *(Obey my instructions but don't copy me)*

Brownie points *(Credit earned as a mark of achievement)*

Keep your nose to the grindstone *(Keep working hard)*

When push comes to shove *(When the pressure is on)*

Out of his depth *(Not having the knowledge)*

Out of his comfort zone *(Not comfortable, not at ease)*

See the writing on the wall
(See signs that there is going to be change)

Be nice to people on the way up because you might meet them on the way down
(Always treat people well in life, you may need their help later)

Pick your brains *(Try to gain some information)*

He who smiles in a crisis has found someone to blame

Nothing succeeds like success
(If you're successful you gain confidence which leads to more success)

To err is human *(Everybody makes mistakes)*

Knuckle under *(Get on with work, stop wasting time)*

Go the extra mile *(Do more than is expected)*

All work and no play, makes Jack a dull boy
(Without time off from work a person becomes dull and boring)

Golden handshake
(A large sum of money given to perhaps encourage retirement)

Golden parachute
(An agreed financial benefit given to someone if employment is terminated)

Think outside the box
(Look at a problem from a different angle)

Asleep at the switch *(Not alert)*

We need some ballpark figures *(We need some general figures)*

Go to the wire *(Go to the extreme to get something done)*

Jump ship *(Leave your job)*

Rat race *(Exhausting, competitive work environment)*

Back to the salt mine *(Return to work)*

People

A knight in shining armour
(Somebody who helps out in time of need)

Alike as two peas in a pod *(Very alike)*

Arm candy *(Attractive person)*

Eye candy *(Attractive person)*

Ankle biter *(Child)*

A sprog *(A child or baby)*

A dog will always return to its own vomit
(A low minded person will always return to the mess he has made)

Barmpot *(A fool)*

A doubting Thomas *(Somebody that doubts everything)*

The big cheese *(An important person)*

Copper-bottomed *(Genuine)*

A bunny boiler
(An obsessive female in pursuit of a lover who has rejected her)

He must have fallen asleep in a greenhouse *(He's very tall)*

Barking mad *(Crazy)*

A skunk at a garden party *(Unwanted guest, to feel out of place)*

Spit happens *(On a baby's bib)*

A constant guest is never welcome

A fool at forty is a fool indeed
(If he hasn't matured by 40 he never will)

A woman's work is never done

Books and friends should be few but good

A man is as old as he feels, and a woman as old as she looks

Fish and guests smell in three days

A big shot *(An important person)*

There's nowt' so queer as folk *(People can be strange)*

A mover and shaker *(Someone who is respected)*

Kissing cousin *(A relative but not a close one)*

A rich man's joke is always funny

Jockey for position *(People struggling for the same position)*

A caution *(A funny person)*

Job's comforter
(Someone who says they want to comfort you but actually do the opposite)

A pain in the butt *(A person who causes problems)*

Naked as a jaybird *(Naked)*

Crazy as a June bug *(Crazy)*

Like a bag of cats *(A bad tempered person)*

You're not so green as you are cabbage looking
(You're smarter than I thought)

All thumbs *(Clumsy)*

A bad egg *(A bad person)*

A couch potato
(Someone who sits on the sofa watching television continually)

A memory like an elephant *(Never forgets)*

Biggest duck in the puddle
(Most important person in the group)

Tall drink of water *(Someone who is tall and slender)*

Sharp cookie *(Not easily fooled)*

Johnny on the spot *(Someone who is always available)*

Smart Alec *(Conceited person who likes to show off)*

Keen bean *(Very studious person)*

Fleet of foot *(Very quick on your feet)*

Shrinking violet *(Shy person)*

A wet blanket *(Someone who doesn't want to join in the fun)*

A bookworm *(Someone who reads a lot)*

Average Joe *(Average person)*

Billy no-mates *(Lone male)*

Norma no-mates *(Lone female)*

Cautionary Clichés

Treading on eggshells *(Being very careful what you say)*

In the doghouse *(In disfavour or trouble)*

To skate on thin ice *(Taking a big risk)*

Burning the candle at both ends *(Staying up too late)*

Don't rock the boat
(Don't upset people by changing the situation)

In the heat of the moment
(Not thought through, something said whilst excited)

Out of the frying pan into the fire
(From one bad situation to another)

Pride comes before a fall
(If you are too confident something will happen, to show you are not as clever as you think)

A shot in the dark
(An attempt to guess something when you have no idea)

What goes around comes around
(If a person does something bad then something bad will happen to them)

I am keeping my eye on you
(To watch over or look after someone)

Up the creek without a paddle *(In a bad situation)*

Between a rock and a hard place *(In a difficult situation)*

Sow seeds of doubt *(Introduce feelings of doubt)*

A hornet's nest *(A situation involving a lot of conflict)*

Don't cross the bridge until you get to it
(Don't anticipate something before it happens)

It's easy to be brave from a safe distance

If it isn't chicken it's feathers *(There is always a problem)*

Discretion is the better part of valour
(Be courageous but not reckless)

Batten down the hatches *(Prepare for bad times)*

You're toast! *(You're in trouble)*

An earbashing *(A scolding)*

Easy!

A piece of cake

As easy as pie

Easy peasy lemon squeezy

Like taking candy from a baby

As easy as falling off a log

Bob's your uncle *(That's it! Problem solved!)*

As easy as duck soup

Easy come, easy go

It's a breeze

Easy on the eye *(Attractive)*

Take it easy

Easier said than done

Easy does it

Easy as beans

Easy as ABC

Pearls of Wisdom

You'll soon find your feet
(You will feel more comfortable with the task in hand)

Six of one and half a dozen of the other *(It's the same)*

Same difference *(There's no difference)*

Out of sight out of mind *(Easily forgotten)*

A truer word was never spoken
(To strongly agree with someone)

That's water under the bridge
(In the past and no longer important)

A wild goose chase *(A futile search)*

Birds of a feather flock together
(People with similar interests tend to stick together)

When in Rome do as the Romans do
(Visitors should try and do as the locals do)

Don't bite the hand that feeds you
(Don't criticise someone who has helped you)

There and back to see how far it is
(A flippant reply that provides no information)

Don't dream your life, live your life
(Don't spend your time dreaming)

Dream as if you'll live forever, live as if you only have today

The moment may be temporary but the memory is forever

If you aren't living on the edge you're taking up too much space
(You need to take a few more risks)

If you lie down with dogs you'll get up with fleas
(Associate with the wrong people and there will be consequences)

A little is better than none
(Better to have something than nothing)

Fortune favours the brave
(Be courageous, go for your goals)

A good conscience is a soft pillow
(A virtuous person will always sleep well, with no need to worry)

A thing of beauty is a joy forever

Beauty is but skin deep
(Beauty does not mean somebody is a good person)

Cheats never prosper
(It's always better to be honest)

Empty vessels make most noise
(Empty headed people are louder than thoughtful people)

Fool me once, shame on you; fool me twice, shame on me

There's no fool like an old fool

Necessity is the mother of invention
(If you need something you will be motivated to provide it)

A bad penny always turns up
(Mistakes always return to haunt us)

A trouble shared is a trouble halved
(Always helps to talk about problems)

Believe nothing of what you hear and only half of what you see
(You should not take everything to be true)

Better to be envied than pitied

Opportunity seldom knocks twice
(Take the opportunity when it arises)

Advice is least heeded when most needed

There will be tears before bedtime
(When something is certain to go wrong)

Fiddle while Rome burns
(Do nothing while disaster strikes)

Knock 'em Dead

Nothing is certain but death and taxes

Kick the bucket

Bite the dust

Look like death warmed up *(To look ill)*

Dead as a doornail

Pushing up the daisies

Dead as a dodo

At death's door *(Really unwell)*

Dead to the world *(Fast asleep)*

Matter of life and death *(Very important)*

Graveyard shift *(Working late at night)*

Over my dead body *(It's not going to happen)*

Outlandish sayings

A duke's mixture *(An odd combination)*

A sack of hammers *(A heavy object)*

Jim dandy *(A fine piece of work)*

All over hell's half acre *(Everywhere)*

For a dog's age *(A long time)*

Give no quarter *(Drive a hard bargain)*

Get your ducks in a row *(Get organised)*

Get your feathers in a bunch *(Get angry)*

Diddly squat *(Nothing)*

Even a blind pig can find an acorn
(Keep trying and you may succeed)

Gone fishing *(Unaware of what is happening)*

Juggle frogs *(To do something that is difficult)*

A drop in the bucket *(A small part, insignificant)*

A bone to pick *(Something to discuss)*

A one horse-town *(A small town where nothing much happens)*

He looked like a pig on ice *(He looked uncomfortable)*

As plain as a pikestaff *(Obvious)*

Even a blind man on a galloping horse could see it
(Plain to see)

That's a tough row to hoe *(A difficult situation)*

Haven't seen you in a month of Sundays
(Haven't seen you for a long time)

There's a dead cat on the line *(Something is wrong)*

As often as a goose goes barefoot *(All the time)*

Big enough to choke a hog *(Very big)*

Big enough to shade an elephant *(Very big)*

Lose your lunch *(Vomit)*

Off your chump *(Crazy)*

Do a Lord Lucan *(Someone who disappears without trace)*

Like getting blood from a stone *(Very difficult if not impossible)*

Muck or nettles *(All or nothing)*

Behind the eight ball *(In a bad situation)*

Happy as Larry

Happy as a box of birds

Happy as a dam in high tide

Happy as a flea in a doghouse

Happy as a fly in pie

Funny as a barrel of monkeys *(Really funny)*

Happy as ducks in Arizona *(Not happy!)*

Salad days *(Happy part of your life, usually youth)*

Have the last laugh *(Win after apparent defeat)*

Laughter is the best medicine

On cloud nine *(Really happy)*

In seventh heaven *(Overjoyed)*

Laugh your socks off *(Laugh heartily)*

Over the moon *(Ecstatic)*

Go ape *(Extremely excited)*

Jump for joy *(Overjoyed)*

No laughing matter *(A serious matter)*

He'd laugh to see a pudding crawl *(Easily amused)*

Shake with laughter *(Laugh uncontrollably)*

Laugh like a drain *(Laugh uncontrollably)*

Mine or Yours?

It's up for grabs *(It's for anyone)*

Bagsy I get first choice *(I said it first so I get first choice)*

Shotgun the telly *(Bagsy the telly)*

I have dibs on the last piece of pie

What's yours is mine and mine's my own

Yoink
(An exclamation that transfers ownership when spoken whilst taking an object from its owner)

Party Fizz!

Paint the town red *(To go out for a lively evening of fun)*

Out on the town *(Go out for the night)*

Let your hair down *(Enjoy yourself)*

Life is for living *(Enjoy life)*

When the cat's away the mice will play
(Without supervision people may misbehave)

It's not so much a barrel of laughs as a vat of vomit

Social butterfly
(Someone with lots of friends always going to social events)

Party animal *(A person who loves parties)*

Crash a party *(Go to a party without being invited)*

A blast *(A great time)*

A live wire *(A fun loving person)*

Stag party *(Party for men, before a marriage)*

Hen party *(Party for women, usually before marriage)*

Embrace your dreams, follow your heart and cherish your life

Life is short......Dance hard!

Dance as if no one were watching
Sing as if no one were listening
And live every day as if it were your last

Alcohol 'isms'

You're not drunk if you can lie on the floor without holding on

A cask of wine works more miracles than a church full of saints

Hit the sauce

Drink like a fish

Absolutely hammered

Had one over the eight

Had a skinful

Three sheets to the wind

Sozzled

Pissed as a newt

Rat-arsed

Tipsy

Legless

As drunk as a skunk

Drunk as a mattress

Drunk as a boiled owl

Drunk as a lord

Tired and emotional *(Drunk!)*

Beauty is in the eye of the beer-holder

Eat drink and be merry

Drown your sorrows

Well-oiled

Pub crawl

Spitting feathers *(Thirsty)*

Hollow legs *(Able to drink a lot)*

A bar fly *(Someone who's always in the bar)*

Champagne taste on a beer budget *(Someone who lives beyond their means)*

Hair of the dog that bit you *(The drink you have the morning after the night before)*

Bottoms up *(Cheers)*

Here's mud in your eye *(Cheers)*

The demon drink *(Alcohol)*

Food for Thought

I could eat the hind legs off a donkey *(Hungry)*

Hungry as a horse

He's a queer fish *(He's a bit strange)*

It's like shooting fish in a barrel *(No challenge)*

Let's go bananas *(Lets go a bit mad)*

Don't try and teach your grandma to suck eggs
(Don't patronise someone older or more experienced)

As sure as eggs *(Absolutely sure)*

Chow down *(Sit down to eat)*

The eye is bigger than the belly

The way to a man's heart is through his stomach

Throw out a sprat to catch a mackerel

Bread is the staff of life

Half a loaf is better than none

If you pay peanuts you get monkeys *(You get what you pay for)*

Curry favour *(Try to get support from people)*

Cheap as chips *(Very cheap)*

Drop him like a hot potato
(Don't have anything to do with him)

A greasy spoon *(A small café that serves fried food)*

Either a feast or a famine *(Either too much or too little)*

Everything from soup to nuts
(From the beginning right to the end)

Best thing since sliced bread *(Really good)*

I'm stuffed *(Couldn't eat any more)*

Pig out *(Devour food greedily)*

Make a pig of yourself *(Eat a lot)*

No picnic *(Not easy)*

Full as a tick *(Well fed)*

A square meal *(A substantial meal)*

Can't do it for toffee *(Absolutely can't do it)*

Put on the feed bag *(Have a meal)*

A fine kettle of fish *(A real muddle)*

Fishy *(Strange, suspicious)*

Full of beans *(Energetic)*

Warm as toast *(Cosy)*

Good Advice

Let not the sun go down on your wrath
(Don't go to bed still angry with someone)

Love of money is the root of all evil
(Money causes lots of problems)

A little knowledge is a dangerous thing
(May cause people to think they know more than they do)

You scratch my back and I'll scratch yours
(You help me and I'll help you)

A watched pot never boils
(If you are waiting for something to happen it seems to take a long time)

Better than a poke in the eye with a burnt stick
(Things could be worse)

Keep it under your hat *(Keep it quiet, don't broadcast it)*

Never put off until tomorrow what you can do today
(Don't procrastinate)

Honesty is the best policy *(Always be honest)*

Speech is silver, silence is golden *(More valuable to say less)*

A loan though old is not a gift *(Still needs to be repaid)*

A day is lost if you haven't laughed

Laughter is the best medicine

Count your blessings *(Be grateful for what you have)*

Experience is the mother of wisdom
(You can only be wise once you have experience)

Better a lie that heals than a truth that wounds
(Kinder to lie than hurt with the truth)

Put your house in order *(Organise your affairs)*

Better late than never *(Better to arrive late than not at all)*

An ounce of prevention is worth a pound of cure
(Try to avoid problems in the first place)

Keep something for a rainy day
(Save for when you may need it)

Least said soonest mended
(Easier to forget a situation once you stop talking about it)

Moderation in all things

Forgive and forget

Eat your words *(Take something back)*

Exclamations

My giddy aunt!

Well I'll go to our house!

I'll go to the foot of our stairs!

Top banana!

Is my eye green?

Was I born yesterday?

I didn't come in on the turnip truck!

Well knock me down and steal my teeth!

Well butter my butt and call me a biscuit!

Well flip me an egg!

I'll be damned!

I'd rather drink bleach!

I'd rather stick pins in my eyes!

Stuff that for a game of soldiers!

Hold your tongue!

Of all the nerve!

Heavens above!

Gordon Bennett!

Gee willickers!

The duck's guts!

You don't know you're born!

Wake up and smell the coffee!

You bet your bippy!

I'll eat my hat!

I'll be a monkey's uncle!

Well knock me over with a feather!

I should cocoa!

For Pete's sake!

Jumping Judas!

Great Scot!

Blood and thunder!

Quirky Quips

What's the deal banana-peel?

What's the deal big wheel?

What's the plan Stan?

What's up Buttercup? *(What's wrong?)*

What's new tennis shoe? *(What's new?)*

See you later alligator In a while crocodile

How now brown cow? *(What's going on)*

How's tricks? *(How are you?)*

Chop, chop lollipop *(Quick now)*

Good night, sleep tight and don't let the bed bugs bite

Irish Idioms & Sayings

People

Who keeps his tongue, keeps his friends *(Don't gossip)*

A friend that can be bought is not worth buying

He's not fit to mind mice at a crossroad *(A useless fellow)*

She has the tongue that would clip a hedge *(A gossip)*

If that man went to a wedding he'd stay for the christening *(Overstay welcome)*

That man could talk the teeth out of a saw *(Very talkative)*

If he's not fishing he's mending his nets *(Plans carefully)*

May your home always be too small to hold all your friends

Life is a strange lad *(Life is seldom straightforward)*

Age is a high price to pay for maturity

Fingerprints make a house a home *(Proof of its inhabitants)*

A nose that would pick a pipe *(A large nose)*

He thinks he's no goat's toe *(He thinks he is better than he is)*

Hell is never full, there is always room for one more
(Be careful, don't run the risk of going to hell)

You're not as young as you used to be,
But you're not as old as you're going to be,
So watch it!

Good man yourself! *(How are you? Or agreement)*

What's the craic? *(Any news?)*

For Good Common Sense

Enough and no waste is as good as a feast

Never bolt your door with a boiled carrot

You may as well give cherries to a pig as advice to a fool

Melodious is the closed mouth

Never rub your eye with anything but your elbow

Never sell a hen on a wet day

There's no point in keeping a dog and barking yourself

Only a fool burns his coal without warming himself

A bad workmen quarrels with his tools

God is good, but never dance in a small boat

It's the quiet pig that eats the meal

Who gossips with you will gossip of you

Poverty waits at the gates of idleness

Laziness is a heavy burden

Chop your own wood and it will warm you twice

A handful of skill is better than a bagful of gold

A heavy purse make a light heart!

If you don't know the way walk slowly

It's no use boiling your cabbage twice

Nodding the head does not row the boat

Better be sparing at first than at last

There are fish in the sea better than have ever been caught
(There is opportunity if you look for it)

You never miss the water 'till the well runs dry
(Something taken for granted until it is no longer there)

Lose an hour in the morning and you'll be looking for it all day
(Use your time wisely)

Honest advice is unpleasant to the ear
(Sometimes we don't like to hear honest advice)

Love & Marriage

No man can prosper without his woman's leave

If you want praise, die, if you want blame, marry

The older the fiddle the sweeter the tune *(Improves with age)*

Blood is thicker than water – and easier seen
(Loyalty to family first)

The best journey always takes us home *(Home is best)*

And to Deal with Misfortune

If God sends you down a stony path, may he give you strong shoes
(May you have the strength to deal with difficult situations)

However long the day, the night must fall
(However bad things are it will look better tomorrow)

There's nothing so bad that it couldn't be worse
(It's bad but it's not so bad)

You'll never plough a field by turning it over in your mind
(Don't keep churning matters over in your head)

A grudge is a heavy thing to carry *(Don't carry a grudge)*

Better be quarrelling than lonesome
(Anything is better than being lonely)

Trouble hates nothing as much as a smile

Patience is a plaster for all sores

Toasts

When the drop is inside the sense is outside

When we drink, we get drunk

As you slide down the banister of life may the splinters never point in the wrong direction

What butter or whiskey does not cure cannot be cured

Here's to those who wish us well and those who don't can go to hell!

> There are many good reasons for drinking,
> One has just entered my head,
> If a man doesn't drink when he's living,
> How in the hell can he drink when he's dead?

Daylight comes through the drunkard's roof the fastest

Men are like bagpipes, no sound comes out from them until they are full

The truth comes out when the spirit goes in

Drunkenness and anger 'tis said tell the truth

He'd step over ten naked women to get to a pint

May your glasses every be full, may the roof over your head be always strong and may you be in heaven half an hour before the devil knows your dead!

> May your neighbours respect you,
> Troubles neglect you,
> The angels protect you,
> And heaven accept you.

> May you live as long as you want
> And never want as long as you live

It's the first drop that destroys you, there's no harm at all in the last

> Here's to a long life and a merry one,
> A quick death and an easy one,
> A pretty girl and an honest one,
> A cold beer and another one!

Drunk is feeling sophisticated when you can't say it

> Here's champagne to your real friends
> And real pain to your sham friends

Friendship's the wine of life; let's drink to it and of it

> The Lord gives us our relatives,
> Thank God we can choose our friends

Here's to being single,
Drinking doubles,
And seeing triple!

I have known many,
And liked not a few,
But loved only one,
And this toast is to you

I drink to your health when I'm with you,
I drink to your health when I'm alone,
I drink to your health so often,
I'm starting to worry about my own!

If it's drowning you're after, don't torment yourself with shallow water

For every wound a balm
For every sorrow, cheer
For every storm a calm
For every thirst, a beer

May the wind at your back always be your own

May the good Lord take a liking to you, but not too soon

Here's hoping you live forever and mine is the last voice you hear

Australian Idioms & Slang

Exclamations

That's beaut!

Bewdie! *(Approval)*

She'll be apples *(She'll be ok)*

No worries

No drama

She'll be right *(OK, fine, no bother)*

You little beauty! *(Cry of approval)*

Go bite your bum *(Be quiet)*

Bloody oath *(That's true)*

That's bonza! *(That's great!)*

Buckley's chance *(No chance)*

Heaps *(A lot)*

Daggy *(Looks bad)*

Good on ya! *(Well done)*

Stiff cheddar *(Bad luck)*

Fair dinkum *(True, genuine)*

Better than a slap in the face with a wet fish
(Better than nothing)

Clear as mud *(Not clear)*

By jingo!

Strewth!

Hooly-dooly *(Expression of surprise)*

Bonza! *(Very good)*

Belt up! *(Be quiet)*

Turn it up! *(Disbelief)*

Don't get your knickers in a knot! *(Don't upset yourself)*

Make like a shepherd and get the flock out of here *(Let's go)*

Not my bowl of rice *(Not for me, not my thing)*

Colder than a penguin's chuff *(Cold)*

Dim-witted

He's got a few roos loose in the top paddock

Too slow to keep worms in a tin

Sharp as a beach ball

A few bricks shy of a full hod

Few tiles short of a roof

Not the full quid

Three bangers short of a barbie

A fruit loop

A drongo

Lamb-brained

A dipstick

Couldn't fight his way out of a paper bag

Couldn't run a bath *(No good at organising)*

Couldn't drive ducks to water *(Useless driver)*

He couldn't get a kick in a cow's yard *(Useless footballer)*

Cheap Shots

A bushpig *(An ugly woman)*

He had a head on him like a sucked mango *(Ugly)*

A face like a smashed crab *(Ugly)*

Rough as bags and twice as nasty *(Uncouth)*

She thinks her feet don't smell
(She thinks she's better than she is)

Your face is like a twisted Ugg boot *(Insult)*

Yer talking Flemington confetti! *(You're talking rubbish)*

All froth and no beer *(Full of himself)*

Flash as a rat with a gold tooth *(Someone who's flash)*

Cunning as a dunny rat *(Very cunning)*

All over the place like a drunken spider *(A state of chaos)*

Mates, buddies

Bloke *(Aussie mate)*

True blue *(Really Australian)*

Built like a brick shithouse *(Strong)*

A cobber *(A mate)*

His blood's worth bottling *(He's a good bloke)*

Mate's rate *(Cheaper than usual for a friend)*

Moolah *(Money)*

The lucky country *(Australia)*

An Aussie *(Someone from Australia)*

Beer & Vittles

Amber fluid or amber nectar *(Beer)*

A billy *(A can for boiling water on the camp fire)*

To put the billy on *(Put the kettle on)*

A chook *(A chicken)*

Grog with no nectar *(Alcohol free beer)*

Throw another shrimp on the barbie *(Quote by Paul Hogan)*

Full as a fairy's phonebook *(Full of grog)*

Full as a boot *(Drunk)*

Crack a tinnie *(Open a can of beer)*

A mystery bag *(A sausage)*

To drink with the flies *(To drink alone)*

A Motley Mixture

Mad as a cut snake *(Upset)*

Flat out like a lizard drinking *(Busy)*

He's having a Barry Crocker *(A bad time)*

He'd make a cat laugh *(He's really funny)*

Mad as a meat axe *(Mad)*

He's a broken packet of biscuits
(All right on the outside but inside a mess)

Cross as a frog in a sock *(Angry)*

Grinning like a shot fox *(Very happy, smug)*

Don't come the raw prawn with me mate
(Don't treat me like a fool)

Belly full of arms and legs *(Pregnant)*

Chuck a wobbly *(Throw a tantrum)*

Free Willy *(Male not wearing underwear)*

He's a pain in the Gregory Peck *(He's a pain in the neck)*

Pommy or Pom *(Someone from England)*

A greenie *(An environmentalist)*

A Sheila *(A woman from Australia)*

Greetings

Owyergoing?

G'day

Cheerio

Toodle-oo

Sundry Sayings

Off like a robber's dog *(Quick)*

Beyond the black stump *(A long way away)*

Chuck a sickie *(Take a day off when you are not ill)*

Up at a sparrow's fart *(Up early in the morning)*

Take a shuftee *(Take a look)*

A hottie *(A hot water bottle)*

Jocks *(Undies)*

Reg Grundy's *(Undies)*

In the nuddy *(Naked)*

This arvo *(This afternoon)*

I'll light the Nelly McGuire *(I'll light the fire)*

Dead ringer *(Very similar)*

Dead cert *(A sure winner)*

Sticky beak *(Inquisitive person)*

Oldies *(Parents)*

Wrinklies *(Senior citizens)*

Crack a fruity *(Go crazy)*

Big bickies *(Expensive)*

Square the circle *(Attempt the impossible)*

Spit the dummy *(Throw a tantrum)*

Sunnies *(Sunglasses)*

Trackie dacks *(Tracksuit pants)*

A scratchie *(An instant lottery ticket)*

Chockie *(Chocolate)*

To vomit

A rainbow sneeze

A kerbside quiche

A Technicolor yawn

A liquid laugh

Pavement pizza

American Restaurant Jargon

Bubble dancer *(Dish washer)*

A blonde with sand *(Coffee with cream and sugar)*

A cup of mud *(A cup of coffee)*

A cup of Joe *(A cup of coffee)*

OJ *(Orange juice)*

Baby juice *(Milk)*

White cow *(Vanilla milkshake)*

Adam and Eve on a raft *(Two poached eggs on toast)*

A spot with a twist *(Cup of tea with lemon)*

Adam's ale *(Water)*

Boiled leaves *(Tea)*

Bucket of cold mud *(Bowl of chocolate ice cream)*

Baled hay *(Shredded wheat)*

Burn one *(Put a hamburger on the grill)*

Burn the British *(Toasted English muffin)*

Check the ice *(Look at the pretty girl who has just come in)*

Cow feed *(Salad)*

Dusty miller *(Chocolate pudding sprinkled with powdered malt)*

Eve with a lid on *(Apple pie)*

Flop two *(Two fried eggs)*

Foreign entanglements *(Spaghetti)*

Frog sticks *(French fries)*

Gravel train *(Sugar bowl)*

Hail *(Ice)*

Hold the hail *(No ice)*

Haemorrhage *(Tomato ketchup)*

High and dry *(A plain sandwich without butter or mayo)*

Hockey puck *(Hamburger, well done)*

Honeymoon salad *(Lettuce alone)*

In the alley *(Served as a side dish)*

Irish turkey *(Corned beef and cabbage)*

Keep off the grass *(No lettuce)*

Love apples *(Tomatoes)*

Mayo *(Mayonnaise)*

Mike and Ike *(Salt & pepper)*

Million on a plate *(A plate of baked beans)*

Nervous pudding *(Jelly)*

Noah's boy on bread
(Ham sandwich – Ham was Noah's second son)

Pigs in a blanket *(Sausage sandwich)*

Pope Benedict *(Eggs Benedict)*

Rabbit food *(Lettuce)*

Radio *(Tuna sandwich)*

Sea dust *(Salt)*

A soup jockey *(A waitress)*

Sunny-side up *(Eggs fried but not flipped over)*

Twelve alive in a shell *(A dozen raw oysters)*

Warts *(Olives)*

Windmill cocktail *(Glass of water)*

Sand *(Sugar)*

Zeppelin *(Sausage)*